Electroneum: The Road To Mass Adoption

By

Anthony E. Joseph

Electroneun

Table of Contents

Introduction 3

Chapter One 6

What is cryptocurrency? 6

Chapter Two 16

What is an ETN? 16

History of Electroneum 19

Future of Electroneum 21

What makes Electroneum different? 24

Why People May Demand This Currency 25

Chapter Three 27

Why you need to invest in Electroneum (ETN) 27

How to Mine Electroneum 31

What is Mining? 32

Electroneum Mining Rewards and Electroneum Mining Difficulty 34

Different Ways to Mine Electroneum 36

Getting Started Mining Electroneum 38

Offline Wallet Set Up 39

Chapter Four 45

Crypto Currency in The Future 45

Should I invest in Cryptocurrencies? 51

Conclusion 53

Electroneum

Introduction

What do you think about technology in the world of finance? Do you think it is something that makes a world of difference? Or it is just one of those inventions that don't matter. Regardless of what you think about technology in finance, one thing is sure it has come to stay. Right now, there are various ways through which you can get money and invest it but, in this book, I will introduce you to the most fantastic way through which you can get the best of both worlds; technology and finance.

You must have heard about cryptocurrencies and how it works. However, what you are offered here is a comprehensive guide to everything about cryptocurrencies. You will be amazed at all the things you didn't know about crypto coins and all the opportunities that abound for you with the digital coins. Now this book isn't like the regular books you've read on finance; I'm going to be giving you a twist that will help you become more proactive with everything you will learn here.

Electroneum

I want you to have an open mind as you read on; think of yourself as a person who doesn't know anything about the subject matter. Cryptocurrencies aren't a new trend, and some inventions have taken place since its inception; as such, it will be difficult to say that one has a firm grip on all the updates. With this book, you get to stay updated, and you also have a first-hand experience of all the things you can do with crypto coins and the world of digital finance.

There are a lot of materials out there about cryptocurrencies, and I have heard some individuals complain bitterly about a lack of understanding of the concept. They also complain about not achieving success with crypto investments. I thought about all of these and arrived at this conclusion; if people do their part by being proactive with what they read, they will achieve results.

I say the same thing to you here; don't just read, implement! Every chapter brings something new to

Electroneum

you, every word is pregnant with meaning, and you will be able to unravel the meaning when you take action. You don't have to worry about complexities either; the book is as easy yet impactful as anything you have ever read. Alright enough of the small talk, it's time to flip through to the next section and begin this fantastic journey to financial freedom with cryptocurrencies. Ready? Let us start.

Electroneum

Chapter One

What is cryptocurrency?

We cannot begin the journey assuming that you know what cryptocurrencies are about so let us start from that point, shall we? Cryptocurrencies are digital currencies; they are not like fiat currencies neither are they like the regular monies you handle on a daily basis. Crypto coins are managed and controlled by technology, and they have been around for a long while. When you think about cryptocurrencies, think of the money you that goes beyond borders and is utilized by a large number of people across the network. So how exactly did cryptocurrency come about?

The very first cryptocurrency which is the Bitcoin was created in 2009 by a developer known as Satoshi Nakamoto in 2009. Since that invention, several other crypto coins have emerged thus making the digital world of finance quite competitive and flexible. Now, the beautiful thing about this is the fact

Electroneum

that unlike other sectors that have been static from inception, the cryptocurrency space has experienced significant improvement in the area of invention. After the Bitcoin, more and more cryptos emerged and it has created a world of possibility for users around the globe.

Cryptocurrencies are digital monies that are cheaper, quicker and way more reliable than government controlled funds. The process of transacting with cryptocurrencies is transparent because every transaction carried out by anyone is placed in the public ledger. This ledger contains the details of every operation done thus making it very open to anyone who wants to get involved with crypto coins. As a user of the crypto-coin, you have full control of your money; you can store your coins yourself and also decide when to transact. You don't have to fill out a form or visit a banking institution. How cool is that?

Security is one of the most favorable features of cryptocurrencies; it is a very secure means of transacting, and there is a unique technology that backs up the system; it is called cryptography. Cryptography or "crypto" for short is the backbone that gives assurance of safety to people who use cryptocurrencies. With the technology, you can be sure that all of your transactions are safe and your investment is in good hands. Because cryptocurrencies are done online, there is always apprehension amongst users, but with cryptography, the fear of an online crash is allayed. Security is still a significant consideration, and with cryptocurrency, you've got that covered.

Anonymity is yet another factor you will bask in when you become an investor. Did you know that when you utilize cryptocurrencies, you can stay anonymous? Oh yeah, it's true. You don't have to reveal your real names. This level of anonymity makes it even more unique thus anyone can get online and transact knowing that the details of their transactions are safe

Electroneum

from other people. When we get to the chapter that deals with how you can buy or invest in cryptocurrencies, you will gain insight into how the whole anonymity aspect works.

The fact that individuals have to deal with third parties when they transact with regular banks is often a source of worry. This intrusion from third parties stifles the transfer of funds from the sender to recipient. With cryptocurrencies, there are no third parties. Whatever transaction you carry out on the platform is done directly with the parties. More so, the directness of the transaction, makes cryptocurrencies one of the fastest means through which money can be transferred. You can move funds from wherever you are to someone in another country with the assurance that the person gets the funds in time.

The cryptocurrency transaction process is a combination of a network of peers; every peer records the history of the transaction and balances the accounts. This is how it works; a person request for a trade, the deal is broadcasted to the P2P network which is consists of computers known as nodes. The network nodes validate the operation as well as the status of the user using algorithms. After the verification process is completed, the transaction with other transactions creates a new block of data on the ledger. The information that is placed on the ledger is permanent and inalterable; at this stage the operation is complete.

A cryptocurrency is a software that anyone can download for free. You don't have to get permission from third parties, founders or authoritative persons. No one can stop you from sending or receiving coins on the platform, so that means you are in control all the time. The primary issue with dependence on the currencies you've got in your country is the lack of stability; the dollar can fluctuate at any time, right? However, cryptocurrency users in these countries

Electroneum

with a smartphone and internet can begin to diversify their wealth by investing in crypto coins.

There are three keywords I want you to have in mind when you think about cryptocurrency in the modern world; reliability, speed, and security. In the world of finance, one word reigns supreme, and that is payment! But more importantly, people are thinking about how they can transact and make payments that are secure, reliable and fast. Cryptocurrencies are reliable because everything about the system is open to all participants and because you control what you do with your coins, you can be sure that you send and receive funds to and from the right persons.

The speed with cryptocurrency means you can transfer funds to a recipient and the person gets it immediately it is confirmed. Those times you had to wait for several days before approving a transaction are over. Cryptocurrencies bring in a new level of speed that can only be achieved with the kind of technology it uses. Once you purchase cryptocurrencies and put them in your wallet. So once you are buying your crypto coins, you can sell and invest them speedily due to the speed of technology.

Security is another feature that makes cryptocurrency the best form of money you can use. Whatever is backed by technology has got a chance at being sustainable. Missing funds, wrong recipient and regular hacks on the system which is familiar with fiat currencies do not happen with cryptocurrencies. Wouldn't you instead utilize a platform that is secure? Once transactions are safe, it puts the mind of the participants at rest.

As at 2017, over a thousand cryptocurrencies exist showing the incredible rate at which they are being accepted. Talking about acceptability, there were issues concerning the level of acceptance people had for cryptocurrencies and this stifled its spread across various countries. However, the level of growth and consistency it has contributes to the speed with which cryptos are used. At first, all you could do with your coins was hold them in your wallet till it was a good time to sell. Now you don't have to hold back in your wallet; you can do so much more with your crypto and gain massive returns on investment. The more governments try to regulate the use of cryptocurrencies; the more interested individuals get because everyone is about natural solutions.

Cryptocurrencies are not used within banking halls or government institutions; the internet is the home that plays host to its transactions. Currently, the total market capitalization of cryptocurrencies is more than $200 billion, and the daily volume is more than $500 billion. Such unprecedented successes can only be recorded by an entity with users that increase every day. With over 3500 growing cryptocurrencies worldwide, you can bet your money on the fact that cryptos aren't going anywhere anytime soon. There is still so much for you to learn and grow with and as we

Electroneum

continue on this journey, you will be able to unravel all that crypto coins have in store for you.

Do you hate all the bank fees that come with carrying out a transaction? Are you often perplexed concerning the amount is taken from your bank account for purchases? With cryptocurrencies transaction fees are minimal compared to what you are charged with at the moment. In 2017, there were transaction fees set at $0.33; this endears more users to the platforms. Also, transaction fees from crypto depend on the supply of network capacity and the demand from the holder of the currency.

It is possible to exchange cryptocurrencies with fiat currencies in some particular online markets. This means you can enjoy exchange rate with world currencies such as British Pounds European Euro and Japanese Yen. However, the exchange rates depend on the present scale where you reside and the typical financial issues you experience there. At first, it

Electroneum

wasn't possible to exchange with fiat currencies, but it is gradually becoming possible because more and more people are accepting the possibility of digital currencies.

Cryptocurrencies may not be able to replace fiat currencies entirely, but they do have the ability to play a complementary role such that there is less pressure on banking institutions and more ease with payments and investments. So think about a world where you have more reliable, safer and faster options to make payment and invest. That you no longer have to rely on your traditional bank methods is enough relief for anyone. This is what cryptocurrency has brought to us today.

This chapter has been a very concise introduction into the world of cryptocurrencies. It is very crucial for you to gain an understanding of the fundamental concepts and how it works before we take another step. I believe you now have a firm grip on what to

Electroneum

expect with cryptocurrencies in general; whatever you find in other chapters will be related to everything you have read here because this is the foundation on which all additional information lies. The next chapter will be all about Electroneum and the history behind the digital coin; this chapter takes our journey to another level, and I cannot wait for you to begin.

Chapter Two

What is an ETN?

Electroneum is a complementary currency that has been developed to allow anyone, regardless of technical ability, easy access to a cryptocurrency. Within a few minutes of installing the mobile app any user can see Electroneum being added to their wallet via the unique mobile mining experience. Nearly all cryptocurrencies are "mined" with specialist equipment. Electroneum can be obtained via the mobile mining experience on the app.

Electroneum's unique mobile mining experience allows anyone with a smartphone to earn ETN coin by letting the miner app run in the background.

Being a cryptocurrency, Electroneum is created, held and spent electronically, and has no physical coins. And since it is guarded by the blockchain, it is not controlled or regulated by any single person, company, or government, but rather by the collective community.

Instead, transactions are processed and validated by a network of thousands of computers around the world (called miners) that must all agree on the account balances of every user. Mathematical functions safeguard every aspect of the process and make sure that no one can game the system or commit fraud.

Traditionally, mining could only be performed on a computer with lots of processing power. However, the Electroneum team has created an algorithm that allows anyone with a mobile phone to mine effectively – thereby making it possible for millions of smartphone users around the world to learn about cryptocurrencies and mine their own coins.

With the launch of Electroneum's Instant Payments System in September 2018, users can now make transactions between one another and get instant payment confirmation. No need to wait for blockchain confirmations.

In traditional cryptocurrencies such as Bitcoin, transactions could take up to an hour to be fully captured in the blockchain. Therefore, they are not suitable for making everyday transactions such as buying groceries at a local store. However, Electroneum acts as a trusted third party between buyer and seller and allows transactions to be confirmed instantly (no waiting time).

Here's how it works:

When a buyer sends ETN to a seller for goods or services, Electroneum checks to make sure the buyer has the required funds available, reserves the funds so it can't be spent again, and then gives instant

Electroneum

confirmation to both parties that the transaction ca be concluded.

Electroneum then gets to work in the background t transfer the funds from the buyer to the seller. Th transfers happen on the blockchain itself. If transaction should fail for whatever reason Electroneum will try again and again until i succeeds.

History of Electroneum

The Electroneum ICO reached their hard cap of 4(million dollars during fundraising. Their Githul release was November 1st. However, before the launch of the mobile app, they were hit by ; distributed denial of service (DDoS) attack. The tean had to shut down their servers and work over 2(hours straight to deal with the attack. Eventually after some delay, ICO investors were distributed thei coins and Electroneum continued working toward: their goal of spreading ETN to the masses. Over 69(

million ETN were transferring during the first 24 hours, requiring only 430 ETN in fees.

Electroneum is the first British based cryptocurrency. The team of 12, based in Kent, is led by Richard Ells, the co-founder of SiteWizard and Retortal.com.

The design of the app places emphasis on users using as many offline wallets as possible to store funds. Once the user is ready to make a transaction, the funds can very easily be imported into the digital wallet for use.

Electroneum's unique value proposition lies not in how it's used, but rather how it is mined.

Electroneum is the first cryptocurrency specifically designed for mobile use. With an estimated 2.2 billion smartphones in use, it certainly seems like a demographic worth targeting.

There are many existing online wallets for almost every cryptocurrency available. Most of these services offer mobile apps from which transactions can be made and balances viewed.

Where Electroneum stands out isn't so much the fact that a mobile-oriented crypto is bound to have a much smoother experience on a mobile than those not designed for it. Its defining feature is the fact that it can be mined on mobile. Well, sort of. More on that in a minute.

Its unique selling point is that even a basic user, who would never go to the effort of mining cryptocurrencies on their computer, can benefit by earning ETN with ease.

Future of Electroneum

Electroneum is one of those invesments that rarely gets thrown around much, seeing that it's goal is to broaden the usage of cryptocurrency for the many people around the world, either wanting to get into crypto, for wanting to have a fast reliable way of payment.

The focus of the coin has been to target the 2 billion people that does own a smartphone, but haven't got a bank account, to store their value. Instead of buying gold as a commodity to store value with, digging it down in the backyard, or safely hiding it, the same people could buy, or actually mine their own ETN.

Imagine having your local 7/11 in SE Asia where i have travelled, adopting ETN. 7/11 is where most people pay their bills in the areas that i have travelled; they trust banks so little that their local convenience store is far more trusted in terms of securing their monthly bills have been paid.

Now the same convenience store has to go through the bank, to process payments made from credit cards or even from ordinary cash the customers pay with. These transaction fees can cost quite a bit in the long run, and has to be offset, by a fee taken from the users credit card, or a small increase in the prices of commodities in that same store.

Electroneum

ETN is the solution to that; with a great model to get adopted into the convenience store, having benefits for both the users and the store owner.

They can even mine their own coins, and get something for free from that same store, with the store owner getting paid for that item; increased revenue, for no cost for anyone at all.

If those people would rather use Electroneum than having to store cash, frightened from getting it stolen or just would prefer it over how easy it is, we have a game changer. Likewise if they wanted to convert the cash they get from working, into ETN or even get paid in ETN, that is where the value lies in addition to letting the people mine.

On the other hand the store owner would be incentivized to adopt the payment system, and heck even mine himself. The offline wallet offers a great tool for those people without a bank account to actually have only one piece of paper they need to take care off, and hide, instead of a dynamic value-storage in the sense of, the amount of cash and gold hidden fluctuates and needs to be dug up, dug back in or taken out from hiding and hid again. This is all done by a simple QR-code.

What makes Electroneum different?

Electroneum offers something no other cryptocurrency has - the ability to mine with a mobile phone (without it blowing up), and, potentially in the future, the ability to mine with an Xbox or Playstation. This gives Electroneum an amazing advantage over competitors - it is a cryptocurrency that is accessible to everyday mums, dads, and kids for the first time ever. The ability for individuals to easily mine and store a cryptocurrency is a huge step forward in technology and should not be sniffed at. In particular, I think that the ability to mine with gaming consoles is particularly exciting because consoles are constantly connected to a secure Wifi and are more powerful than phones.

Why being accessible to the mass market is important for investors in Electroneum

Electroneum

Put simply, if the mass consumer market is able to hold Electroneum via simple mining (which, given customers will be able to mine from their phone and maybe gaming consoles which for the consumer is essentially free money...), this creates a demand for vendors to offer Electroneum as a payment method. This is particularly applicable to gaming companies and gambling companies, both markets worth tens of billions in annual revenue. There is a huge incentive for anyone who owns a gaming console or a Smartphone to download the app and start mining immediately - it is free cash after all and people would be stupid not to.

Why People May Demand This Currency

Developers will want to gain access to this huge potential marketplace of new currency. Part of the reason they will do this is because if people can buy things (e.g. gambling money or gaming cash) directly from their Electroneum wallets, they will not need to involve themselves in cold storage or other technical areas of cryptocurrency ownership and this is attractive to both the consumer and the developer. For example, in Australia if William Hill opened up their gambling site to accepting Electroneum, I would always deposit any mining amounts earned straight into my William Hill account as this, for me, turns it into cash. William Hill can then choose to pay customers in Electroneum when they withdraw or sell it to other consumers of Electroneum. Additionally, online/mobile gamers will be potentially able to use Electroneum across multiple games, allowing them to pay for virtual currency across multiple games rather than put it all into one for a single purchase. It will also allow them to transfer currency between games, with developers incentivized to allow this with spread commissions. As a mobile gamer, I know I would be much more likely to purchase gaming currency if I could move it later if I got sick of the game.

Electroneum

Chapter Three

Why you need to invest in Electroneum (ETN)

Electroneum (ETN) Target Market

The smartphone industry is massive. It has over 2.2 billion users and it is still growing. This is one of the things that make Electroneum an attractive investment option. Electroneum (ETN) will henceforth be open to an enormous market of users who will have the opportunity to mine and buy tokens with ease.

For new entrant to the world of cryptocurrency that are having trouble joining exchanges; downloading the Electroneum app and trying to win free coins provide an excellent entry point into the world of crypto.

Cryptocurrencies are not that easy for the average users to buy as it usually requires some extra effort.

Electroneum (ETN) aims change this by making the digicoin easier to purchase and mine on mobile apps thereby bringing cyptocurrency to the masses.

Simply put, the coins are mined through a combination of centralized viral marketing app and decentralized blockchain. The blockchain gives out coins to mobile device users who then take along the service of viral marketing to Electroneum through a gamified experience.

Electroneum's (ETN) Instantaneous Transaction Authorization and Multi-crypto payment

Electoneum (ETN) has a patent, for instant payments pending. This patent would revolutionize the cryptospace once it is awarded as it isn't just for ETN alone but other cryptos as well. The ability of being able to spend coins immediately will simply unlock the true value of cryptos as they become usable as everyday currencies.

Electroneum

Another USP (unique selling point) is the instantaneous speed with which transactions made on the Electroneum platform are authorized. Electroneum's instant payment which has gone live allows you to immediately complete a Point of Sale (POS) or online checkout. Instead of having to wait minutes for transactions to show on blockchains or waiting hours for banks to release your funds, Electroneum platform allows recipient to send goods straightaway due to its ability to guarantee the fund.

Due to Electroneum's Hybrid model of both a decentralized blockchain and a centralized app, ETN can immediately confirm to a vendor that an Electroneum user possesses the funds in the wallet. To forestall double spending the Electroneum app ring-fences the sender's fund.

Electroneum (ETN) is KYC (Know Your Customer) Compliant

Its KYC features afford Electroneum (ETN) the opportunity to grow as this feature gives it a factor of legitimacy in the government's eyes. The KYC technology is likely to be on the rise even in the cryptographic space, most especially as both the state and federal regulators intensifies their efforts to clamp down on fraud and close down companies responsible for facilitating their activities.

Currently most governments are dawdling in accepting cryptos as forms of payment as they could be platforms for money laundering, terrorism and other financial crimes. Electroneum, by having KYC has sealed these loopholes thereby making it complaint with most countries financial regulations. The issue of security had been one of the obstacles to the mainstream adoption of crypto and KYC technology– especially solutions that are easy to use and fast- can help to bypass it.

The potential for mass adoption without governmental imposed logjams could see the value of this crypto rise to unparalleled height across the globe. You can be sure that as this adoption takes root so also will the value of Electroneum (ETN) soar.

Electroneum

This same KYC feature also provides it with the opportunity to work with telecoms companies the world over. The telecoms companies would benefit by incorporating Electroneum into their system which would allow their users make instant payment through their smartphones. And incorporating Electroneum into their systems could see this cryptographic project gaining billions of users in relative short time globally.

How to Mine Electroneum

The idea of Electroneum is to make cryptocurrency available to everyone. The team behind the project have created very easy to use software and made it available on lots of different devices. Both mobile phone and computer users can setup the software needed to mine Electroneum with just a few clicks.

Although it's very easy to get started mining Electroneum and users don't need special hardware it can still be a little scary – particularly if you're not a technical type of person!

There's no point mining a coin if you have nowhere to store it! First you'll want to visit my.electroneum.com and create either a paper wallet or an online wallet with the referral code (633585). While a paper wallet is more secure, it's also a bit more complicated for beginners in the crypto world to manage. Your online Electroneum wallet will also require two-factor authentication, a PIN and Captcha verification each time you log in to manage it, so there are added layers of security.

What is Mining?

Before I get started, you first need to understand what mining cryptocurrency actually is.

Mining is the process of verifying transactions between different users of a cryptocurrency. Rather than using a single central authority to check transactions (like a bank), all the network's participants (also known as nodes) check that no user has sent the same coins twice or has cheated the system in any other way.

For doing this work, miners are rewarded with coins. The coins come from a block reward and the fees included with transactions. The fact that miners earn money for the act of mining is important to stop nodes joining together and attacking the network. It simply makes more economic sense to play by the rules than it does to cheat the network.

What is Electroneum Mining?

The special thing about mining Electroneum is how easy it is to get started. Unless you're a coder, if you do a Google search about almost any other cryptocurrency mining, you'll quickly get very confused by the instructions.

The Electroneum team wanted to change this. They wanted to create a cryptocurrency that anyone could mine. This should lead to a more decentralized network and one that is stronger against network attack.

Electroneum uses a special ASIC-resistant mining code. This makes it different from Bitcoin, for example. In Bitcoin, users can use specialized pieces of hardware that are called ASICs (Application Specific Integrated Circuit). These chips are expensive to buy. This makes it impossible for every potential user of Bitcoin to run their own node and mine the currency.

Thanks to the way that Electroneum has been designed, even mobile phones can mine it. It might only make the miner a few cents per day, but when you consider how many people in the world live on less than $2 a day, this can make a big difference.

Electroneum Mining Rewards and Electroneum Mining Difficulty

As mentioned, cryptocurrency miners earn rewards for verifying transactions. These are both the transactions fees, as well as a reward set by the code itself.

The Electroneum mining reward goes to whichever miner (or pool of miners) solves a complex computer problem. If the reward is won by a pool, it is shared between that pool of users. As more and more miners start to attempt to solve this complex problem, there becomes more competition. This means that it gets harder for each individual user to mine successfully.

The current miner reward for Electroneum is 6,413.56 ETN, which is equal to $136 at today's rate.

Any user can win this reward. However, the more processing power (hash rate) a miner has, the more likely they are to solve the problem. Therefore Electroneum mining pools are a good option for users mining on less powerful devices.

The pools work together on the problem and it doesn't matter which individual node solves it. If one member does, the others get a share of the reward. The amount of processing power contributed to the pool will decide how large each users' share will be.

Different Ways to Mine Electroneum

There two main ways to mine Electroneum. Users can choose to solo mine or mine as part of a pool. I've listed the advantages of each below.

Solo Mining

Solo Electroneum mining is only suitable for users with high computing power. For Electroneum, this will mean those with dedicated graphics cards on their computers (GPUs).

The advantages of being a solo miner are that you won't need to pay any fees to the pool itself and there is no middleman. This second point is important because Electroneum mining pools have been hacked in the past.

The disadvantages of being a solo miner is the waiting time for winning a reward. It can take a very long time to earn when mining solo!

You can think of it like working for commission. As a car salesperson, for example, you might work many long days without making a single sale. When you do finally hit one, it's a big payday, but the downtime can get too much for some people. Solo miners can work at the problems for ages and not receive anything. They do get all the reward when they finally do solve one though!

Mining as Part of an Electroneum Mining Pool

For most users, working as part of a Electroneum mining pool is the best option. It gives them consistent rewards and allows them to mine cryptocurrency without having to use special hardware.

Mining pools work like this — you combine your computing power with other people and you are rewarded with the same % of Electroneum as you contribute in power to the pool. So, if you provide 10% of power to the Electroneum mining pool, you will receive 10% of the reward. Simple!

Getting Started Mining Electroneum

The following step by step guides have been prepared to explain how to mine Electroneum to users who have never mined cryptocurrencies before. They are not the most profitable way, but they should serve as an excellent way to introduce people to mining.

Mining Electroneum Using a CPU

First, you need a secure wallet so that you can store your Electroneum once you start the Electroneum mining.

Below I have explained how to create a secure offline wallet. A more functional but less secure wallet can also be created by signing up to Electroneum from their website. This involves giving the company a lot of information about you which some users won't be comfortable with.

Offline Wallet Set Up

The following is a quick guide to setting up an offline wallet.

Head to the <u>downloads</u> section of the Electroneum website.

- Click either "browser version" or "download ZIP". If you're using the browser version, you'll need to make sure you're using Google Chrome. For this demonstration, I'll be using the browser version. For more security, the rest of the guide should be performed offline or ideally on a computer that has never been online.
- Read the disclaimer about private keys on the following page. When you understand about the importance of keeping your private spend key secret, you can click "Let's Get Started".

- Move you mouse around in random patterns on the next screen. This step is to generate a truly random key set.

- Next, read the warning about the importance of keeping the printed wallet safe. When you understand the content on the page, click "Save Wallet as PDF."
- Open the PDF and print the key sets. For a more secure wallet, disconnect your printer from the internet. Better still, use one without memory or wireless connections.

Installing the Beginners Pool Mining Software

Now that you have somewhere to store your mined Electroneum, it's time to install the mining software.

- Head to the downloads section of the Electroneum website again.
- Click on "download windows miner".
- When you've downloaded the software, you might find that either Chrome or your computers anti-virus software stops you from opening it. If this is the case, disable your anti-virus and go into Chrome's settings menu. From there, click the advanced options and

disable the option to "protect you from dangerous sites". Restart the download and you should find that Chrome now lets you open the ".exe" file.

- Once you have opened the Electroneum Pool Miner software, you will find a standard installation menu. Follow the onscreen prompts to add the application to your computer.
- Open the Electroneum Pool Miner and add your ETN wallet address. You will also need to add a number under the number of threads box. For this, you need to know how many cores your computer's processor has.
- Next, you must add the URL of the Electroneum mining pool that you'll be using. We recommend EasyHash for now. Later, you can try other pools.
- Use this format in the URL box: stratum+tcp://[URL]:[port] – you must replace [URL] and [port]. If you're using a low-end CPU use "stratum+tcp://etn.easyhash.io:3630".

Alternatively, for high end CPUS, use "stratum+tcp://etn.easyhash.io:3631"
- Once all the details have been completed, click "start mining".

That's all there is to it.

Mobile Phone Mining

As mentioned earlier, you can also mine Electroneum using a mobile phone. This feature is new and currently it's available on Android and iOS devices. To install the application and register as a user, follow the steps below:

- Visit the Google Play store.
- Search for Electroneum.
- Click "Download", then when it has downloaded click "install".
- Register an account by visiting my.electroneum.com and filling in the information requested.
- Verify your email address by visiting your inbox and clicking the link in it.

- Provide your mobile phone number. Electroneum will then send a code to the number. This stops people creating many different accounts. When it arrives, enter the code into the box on the registration page.
- Provide an alternative email address that restoration details can be sent to if you lose the PIN code for your account.
- Key in a PIN code that you are sure to remember. You will need this every time you launch the app or when sending transactions.
- Finally, head back to your email inbox and click the link in the email sent to you. This confirms that you have received a PIN recovery email. You can now log in to the app.

All you need to do to start Elecetroneum mining now is go down to the box that says, "start mining" and click it.

Is Electroneum Mining Profitable?

The profitability of mining Electroneum is going to depend on quite a few factors. I've listed them below to give you a better idea of whether it will be worth it for you:

- Hash rate: The more powerful your hardware is, the more profitable your mining should be.
- Power consumption: Devices that use less energy are going to be more profitable.
- Cost Per KWh: If you live somewhere with cheap energy, you will have a better chance of making a profit.
- Cost of the hardware.

You can test different configurations of hardware using an online mining profitability calculator.

Is Mobile Mining Profitable?

Since mobile phones are generally much less powerful than CPUs and certainly GPUs, it is unlikely that you will show pure profit mining Electroneum using a mobile phone. However, since the Electroneum platform targets developing nations, mobile mining is an excellent way to save some

Electroneum

money on the cost of owning and using the mobile device in the first place.

Chapter Four

Crypto Currency in The Future

1. Cryptos will disrupt the norms of commerce

The rules of economics will change in the future because of cryptocurrencies. The manner and way we carry out business will be different from the way it is now because technology will take over. There will be more cases of people willing to utilize crypto coins because of the benefits and ease it brings.

As opposed to going to the bank and waiting for long queues more people will slightly transfer speedily to the recipient over the blockchain. Due to the absence of intermediaries, investors will find cryptocurrencies more attractive as it is an opportunity for them to cut cost. Remember that cryptocurrencies offer meager fees for transactions; who wouldn't want to take advantage of this?

2. More investors will buy in

As opposed to experiencing a lack of investments there will be an increased financial investment in cryptocurrencies. The business world will be shaken by the ease with which technology is made easy thus attracting more people in. Before you got a hold of this book, you probably had a lot of doubts about cryptocurrencies, and now those doubts are dispelled because you have the authentic information about crypto coins.

With more investors, crypto coins will circulate in the economy more thus making it a viable form of investing. There is a world of difference between the number of investors that started out with Bitcoins and the number of investors presently pushing funds in cryptocurrencies. There is bound to be an increase in this number because people seek better and more natural ways to get things done.

3. Government attempt at regulation will increase

There will be an increased effort made by the government to regulate cryptocurrencies more than ever before. If you recall I did mention that cryptos aren't restricted currently as such, it will be difficult for the government to demand tax. There is no central authority to request such payments which explains why they will want to get their hands on that sector. The move to regulate cryptocurrencies also steam from the need to control the flow of funds which leads to a slow process (we experience this with the banks all the time)

In the future cryptocurrencies will face the same stiff opposition it experienced in recent years from the government of various countries that haven't accepted its use in their countries. Some things happening now with crypto coins will be carried over to the future, and this is one of them.

4. More retails stores will accept crypto coins

Already, some retail stores accept cryptocurrencies but there is a lot of emphasis on online stores. In the future, there will be more offline stores that key to accepting cryptocurrencies. This is a break down of the analysis; the more people transact with cryptocurrencies; the more organizations have to take because it becomes an option for people.

So we will see a gradual shift from online stores dominating the crypto space to offline stores. So we will get to see more "cryptocurrency accepted here" signs in stores as opposed to the kind of signs we see now. You will be able to shop with your coin whenever you want from a broad selection of stores as well.

5. Insecurity will also be on the increase

With all of these changes taking place, vulnerabilities will be on the rise as well. The more interest increases with crypto coins, the more it draws the attention of fraudsters and hackers. At times like this, you need to take all of the precautions I shared with you on how to create a wallet and store your coins. The level of insecurity will increase, and you will have to watch the way you expose your coins to the internet.

Insecurity is a general phenomenon in the finance world, with everyone trying to get the money it can get crazy as such, with the increase in interest people have for cryptocurrencies, you should also increase the level with which you are alert.

6. A leading alternative to fiat currencies

With cryptocurrencies, we will have an option to fiat currencies. Some futurists believe that cryptocurrencies will take over the central bank and while this remains to be seen, I do think that crypto coins will be a suitable alternative to crypto coins. You may not be able to do everything that fiat currencies do with cryptos entirely, but you will be able to do more things. When a currency is in high demand, it affects other currencies, and this is how it will be for cryptocurrencies.

As an alternative, you will also have more investment options that will yield great returns for you. This also shows that cryptocurrencies will be very relevant in the future; you will begin to see the best in cryptocurrencies.

Should I invest in Cryptocurrencies?

With all you have gleaned, the question above may be troubling your mind. If you want to invest, I advise that you treat it as an investment in the same way you handle other ventures. Recognize that you run the risk of losing it all should anything go wrong. Remember that crypto coins have no intrinsic value other than what the buyer is willing to pay the seller at the point of transacting. As such it is susceptible to price swings which increases your risk. So, you think you can handle the threats; you need to find other forms of investment with minimal risk features.

I wanted you to have a balanced idea of everything about the future of cryptocurrencies. You have a balanced view of getting to know the positives and risks involved. It is better you go into this fully aware of what is to come as opposed to not understanding. Oh yes, the future is bright for cryptocurrencies; so long we still have the technology, we will have digital coins. However, there are real risks and challenges. Be aware of such risk, digest more books and you will know exactly what to do at all times.

This chapter comes to a close here, and so does the book. It has been the most fantastic experience for me, and I hope you can say the same for yourself. There is a concluding page after this; don't roll your eyes thinking you have to reread a lot, I know you need a break. Go to the concluding page and pat yourself on the back for being such a good sport.

Electroneum

Conclusion

What a great journey we have been on! I am still reeling off the significant progress we have made from merely defining the word "cryptocurrency" to learning more about how this digital coin is shaping the world of finance. This book is a definitive guide to all things Electroneum; this means that everything you need to know about this topic has been handled here as such, you can always come back to the pages here for guidance if you ever feel like you didn't get any concept.

The journey with this book comes to an end here, but it isn't the end for you; it is the beginning of greater things to come. I believe the issues have been instrumental in helping you glean more about the concept of Electroneum. Ready to take on the world of cryptocurrencies now? I hear a loud YES! Soar on and win!

Best Wishes.

Electroneum

Electroneum

www.ingramcontent.com/pod-product-compliance
Lightning Source LLC
Chambersburg PA
CBHW031550210526
45464CB00003B/1244